G is for Getaway, made at the run.

H ...ne!

I is for Innocence. See that smug face!

J is for Jam that is gone without trace.

K is for Kidding. Dennis seems bold.

LIONS

DANGER

L is for Lion. It's timid and old!

M is for Magic. This seems a good trick.

MAGIC

N is for No Good. He has to run quick!

Printed and published in Great Britain by D. C. Thomson & Co., Ltd., 185 Fleet Street, London EC4A 2HS.
© D. C. Thomson & Co., Ltd., 2000.
ISBN 0-85116-735-7.

The Dennis the Menace Book, 1968

David Law

David Sutherland

David Parkins

of a hooped jersey added the final touch to a style which made Dennis the original 'punk'.

Dave Law's version of Dennis continued to develop over his twenty year stint as Dennis's pet artist. This changing style is clearly evident in the pages of this book with the mid to late fifties seeing our hero 'grow up' quite literally . . . to an elongated spindly version of the dumpy little rogue who started out.

Once Dennis was brought back down to size, David Law produced much of his best work in the early 1960's. His unique loose style and characteristic low horizons helped make the strip hugely popular with readers of all ages.

Script writing for Law must have been easy — involve a few animals in Dennis's adventures and hilarious pictures were guaranteed.

Scriptwriter Ian Gray came up with a doggy sidekick for Dennis in 1968, asking David Law to base the

Right: Creating the Menace – David Law's pencil roughs for the Dennis The Menace Book 1962. The finished cover can be seen on the right.

AS well as sharing the same Christian name, David Law, David Sutherland and David Parkins share something else in common — they have been the artists charged with bringing Dennis the Menace to life in the pages of "The Beano" over the past 50 Menacing Years.

Dennis broke the mould (and that wouldn't be all he'd break) from previous comic stories when he first appeared in March, 1951. He was the first anti-authority rebel to (dis)grace the pages of a comic. His sole quest was to have as much fun as possible and pompous figures of authority and killjoy parents weren't going to stop him.

Dundee newspaper strip artist David Law was the first to bring the unruly little rascal to life. Dennis's mischievous grin and out-of-control hair gave him the desired look and, after a few weeks, the addition

DAVIDS

Right: The Menace Future? David Parkins has created a virtual Dennis inside his computer.

Left: 50 years of Dennis the Menace – l–r. by Davids Law, Sutherland and Parkins.

DENNIS THE MENACE

Below: Another pencil rough showing how David Law 'built up' a page.

animal on Dennis's hairstyle with legs, eyes and granite-shattering teeth added. So Gnasher was born and it didn't take long for readers to react so positively that Gnasher was signed up as a regular accomplice to Dennis's fun.

In the late 1960's Dave Law's health began to decline and former adventure story artist David Sutherland was called in as understudy on Dennis. David Sutherland's background in advertising and drawing Disney posters, coupled with having illustrated The Bash Street Kids since 1962 gave him the ability to copy Law's style amazingly closely. Sadly, David Law was forced to retire through ill health in 1970 and for the next twenty-eight years Dave Sutherland continued to produce The Beano's two most popular stories, Dennis and The Bash Street Kids, in tandem, somehow managing to maintain two entirely different styles of drawing for the two stories.

By 1974 Dennis had commandeered the front and back covers of The Beano and by 1977 Gnasher's popularity was such that he was given his own "Gnasher's

Below: Gnasher, Dennis's Abyssinian Wire-haired Tripe hound, drawn by David Law (top) and David Sutherland.

Tale" page.

As if that wasn't enough, along came a ripsnorting new pet — a hairy, pink pig called Rasher whose pretty disgusting antics earned him and Dave Sutherland another page in the comic by 1984.

Dennis's fame was spreading and he soon demanded another page in the comic. In November 1993 he was given the first three pages of The Beano to allow him to be an even bigger menace than usual.

With David Sutherland about to take semi-retirement in 1998 (he still produces The Bash Street Kids), a new artist was needed for Dennis. Lincoln artist David Parkins seemed to have the right credentials — he had great versatility . . . and his name was David!

In August 1998 David Parkins took over The Beano's favourite Menace and swiftly introduced a young pretender to Dennis's Menacing throne when he helped design the new addition to the Menace family — Dennis's baby sister, Bea.

As has been the case over Dennis's fifty year history, he continues to grow and grow.

As well as appearing on every form of merchandise imaginable, this year's Beano Book 2001 sees our little terror head off to new galaxies in an innovative, computer-generated story created by David Parkins, bringing The World's Wildest Boy bang up to date.

Gnasher on the front cover of the Beano, February 12th, 2000, as drawn by David Parkins.

DENNIS ACCORDING TO DAD

DENNIS CAUSES BALDNESS — HE'S MADE ME TEAR OUT MY HAIR, ANYWAY! THE NEXT FEW PAGES WILL SHOW YOU SOME OF THE TERRIBLE TROUBLE THAT SON OF MINE HAS CAUSED ME. YOU MIGHT WELL LAUGH, BUT THAT BOY'S COST ME A FORTUNE IN REPAIRS . . . THOUGH HE HAS SAVED ME ON HAIRCUTS, I SUPPOSE.

DENNIS THE MENACE — POOR ME!

This strip appeared in The Beano issue dated 8th December, 1962

I'VE TRIED MY BEST WITH DENNIS, REALLY I HAVE. ANYTHING I COULD DO TO MAKE HIM A LITTLE MORE, WELL, **NORMAL**, I'VE GIVEN IT A SHOT, STARTING WITH ELOCUTION LESSONS . . .

I'M TAKING YOU FOR VOICE-TRAINING LESSONS. YOUR SPEECH IS AS SLOVENLY AS THE REST OF YOU!

AW, DAD, NO!

DENNIS NOW MEETS HIS TEACHER, MR HORACE TAWKE.

DEE-LIGHTED TO MEET YOU, DEAR BOY!

RATS TO YOU, MATE!

OOH! WHAT DREADFUL SPEECH!

SHUDDER!

FIRST YOU MUST LEARN TO PRONOUNCE THE VOWELS CORRECTLY. REPEAT AFTER ME, A-E-I-O-U!

AEIOU!

AGH!

BUT BRAVELY HORACE CONTINUES WITH THE LESSON.

SAY "HOW NOW, BROWN COW?"

HOW NOW, BROWN COW?

EEK!

TRY SAYING, "THE RAIN IN SPAIN FALLS MAINLY ON THE PLAIN." GULP!

NERVE PILLS

THE RAIN IN HERE FALLS MAINLY ON YOU, TEACHER, DEAR. HEH! HEH!

YO-YO

CRACK!

WHIRR!

SPLASH!

WHOOSH!

CLOCKWORK FAN

OOH! EEK! STOPPIT, YOU HORRID CHILD!

ATER—

I'D BETTER GO AND SEE HOW DENNIS IS GETTING ON!

HEH-HEH! DEE-LIGHTED TO SEE YOU, FATHER, DEAR!

WHAT HAVE YOU DONE TO MR TAWKE? HE'S SPEECHLESS!

SPEECHLESS

LOOK, READERS, DENNIS IS PRACTISING HIS VOWELS.

AEIOU!

"THE SLIPPER OF DAD FALLS MAINLY ON HIS LAD."

14th October, 1961

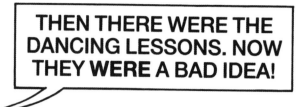

THEN THERE WERE THE DANCING LESSONS. NOW THEY **WERE** A BAD IDEA!

CRASH!

CLATTER!

GOOD GRACIOUS! WHAT'S GOING ON IN DENNIS'S ROOM?

YOU CLUMSY, AWKWARD LOUT! STOP IT THIS INSTANT!

GOAL

THUD!

CLUMP!

WHAT A DREADFUL BOY!

A-ONE AND A-TWO AND AN UPWARD KICK! HEH! HEH!

EEK!

BONK!

NOW, I WANT YOU ALL TO TWIRL GRACEFULLY —SO!

RIGHT! I'LL SHOW THEM A TWIRL ALL RIGHT!

COME HERE TILL I SPANK YOU!

NOT LIKELY! A-ONE AND A-TWO AND A-*HUP!*—

GRACEFUL LEAP

—AND A-TWO AND A-CHEERIO, DAD!

COME BACK!— AGH!

CRASH!

YOU CLUMSY MAN! YOU'RE WORSE THAN THE BOY!

GROAN!

HE HE!

DANCE TIME

20th October, 1962

2nd January, 1982

THE GUARD DOG SEEMED TO BE A GOOD IDEA.
BARK!

GNASHER DOESN'T LIKE OTHER DOGS IN THE HOUSE—

YOWL!
—HE DOESN'T MIND THEM IN TREES, THOUGH!

NEXT WE TRIED A BATALLION OF SOLDIERS!

CLUMP!
CLUMP!
CLUMP!

WAIL!
SOB!
PEAS
STINK BOMBS
I HATE TO SEE GROWN MEN CRY!

Later— LOOKS LIKE WE WON'T BE ABLE TO GO TO THE DANCE.

OH, NO! IT'S GEORGE MILD FROM THE OFFICE!
ER-G-GOOD M-MORNING, IF YOU DON'T MIND ME SAYING SO!

WHY, GEORGE—MAYBE YOU COULD DO ME A FAVOUR!
WHY, OF COURSE! ANYTHING! CERTAINLY!

So—
GEORGE HERE IS GOING TO MIND DENNIS WHILE WE'RE AT THE DANCE!
FEELING FAINT
HAW-HAW-HAW!

Presently— SHOW DENNIS YOUR FASCINATING COLLECTION OF PAPER-CLIPS! HE'S DYING TO SEE THEM!
OOH! I'D LOVE TO!

SO GLAD YOU'RE INTERESTED IN MY LITTLE HOBBY!

After the dance—
THIS IS A VERY RARE MONGOLIAN PAPER-CLIP-DRONE-DRONE—
HOW DID GEORGE GET ON I WONDER?

THEY WERE AS GOOD AS GOLD — DIDN'T SAY A WORD!
SO BORED STIFF THEY FELL ASLEEP
Z-Z-Z-Z!
SNORE!
HEH-HEH! GEORGE HAS THAT EFFECT ON EVERYONE!

November, 1979

6th June, 1953

0th June, 1953.

SAFARI PARKS ARE FUN, BUT WITH DENNIS IN THE CAR, YOU'RE NEVER QUITE SURE WHETHER THE SAFEST PLACE ISN'T OUTSIDE WITH THE ANIMALS!

Weekly News

THERE'S NO STOPPING THAT LAD OF MINE. TAKE FISHING — A RESTFUL, PEACEFUL, NON-MENACING PASTIME, YOU MIGHT THINK. BUT NO! WHEN DENNIS GRABS A ROD, THE ONLY THINGS THAT AREN'T AT RISK ARE THE FISH!

YIPPEE! AUNT BESSIE'S SENT ME A FISHING ROD!

NOW, MUM, DON'T ALWAYS LOOK ON THE GLOOMY SIDE!

GOING UPSTAIRS TO FISH!

ALL RIGHT, DENNIS.

TWO MINUTES LATER —

WHAT AM I DREAMING ABOUT? HOW CAN DENNIS BE GOING FISHING UPSTAIRS?

STOP IT, DENNIS!

HUH! HERE COMES THE SPOILSPORT—AND I COULD HAVE CAUGHT ALL THE PEARS IN THE GARDEN NEXT DOOR!

I'LL TEACH YOU HOW TO CATCH FISH.

HE CAN'T TEACH ME ANYTHING!

STOP!

HAVE YOU BEEN UP TO ANYTHING, DENNIS?

WHO? ME?

LATER — AN OLD BOOT! NEVER MIND. KEEP TRYING.

HUH! THE FISH MUST BE ON HOLIDAY OR SOMETHING!

AN OLD BOOT'S NO GOOD TO ME!

I'LL STAND WELL BACK THIS TIME!

I'M BEGINNING TO LIKE FISHING!

I'D BETTER GET OUT OF THE WAY— OW!

LOOK OUT, DAD! I'VE CAUGHT SOMETHING ELSE!

IT WAS GOOD OF YOU TO HOOK AN OLD SLIPPER, DENNIS!

THERE'S ALWAYS A CATCH!

The Weekly News

HONESTLY! YOU DO YOUR BEST TO HELP DENNIS OUT OF TROUBLE, AND JUST WHEN YOU THINK HE'S RUN OUT OF IDEAS, SOME 'ORRIBLE RELATION ON HIS MOTHER'S SIDE GOES AND SENDS HIM A RIDICULOUS PRESENT, DESIGNED TO SEND ME BONKERS! BAH!

DAD IS A KEEN AMATEUR CARPENTER—

I'VE NEARLY FINISHED THIS DINING-ROOM SUITE.

BANG!

THEN—

BEAUTIFUL! I'LL TREASURE IT ALWAYS!

GLEAM

BUT DAD'S NOT HAPPY FOR LONG.

LOOK WHAT AUNTIE NELLIE SENT ME, DAD—A TOY JOINER'S SET!

OH! NO! I FEAR THE WORST!

DAD'S NOT DISAPPOINTED.

GOODY! THE SAW WORKS OKAY!

LOOK, FOLKS. TWIN BEDS!

AGH-H! I MUST GUARD MY BELOVED SUITE!

SO—

DENNIS MUST NOT GET NEAR IT!

MEANWHILE.

WELL, I MUST BE GOING. I'M SORRY I WASN'T ABLE TO MEET YOUR DEAR, LITTLE BOY.

EEK!

DRRRR!

HM-M! LOOKS LIKE SHE'S MET HIM NOW!

I WAS JUST TESTIN' MY LITTLE DRILL. HAR! HAR!

WHAT A REVOLTING CHILD!

THROB!

NO MORE OF IT, DO YOU HEAR? GO AND DO YOUR HOMEWORK SUMS!

BANG! BANG! BANG! BANG! BANG! BANG!

SHRIEK! THIS IS THE LAST STRAW!

BANG! BANG!

NAILS

WHAT'S THIS? DAD'S ACTUALLY TEARING HIS PRECIOUS SUITE APART!

I'M NEEDING THE WOOD—

RIP!

CRUNCH!

—TO MAKE A STRONG CRATE—

BANG! BANG!

—TO KEEP MY SON IN!

YOUR SUPPER, DENNIS!

ANGRY MUTTERINGS.

2nd December, 1961

30th December, 1961

DENNIS NEVER MISSES A PHOTO OPPORTUNITY

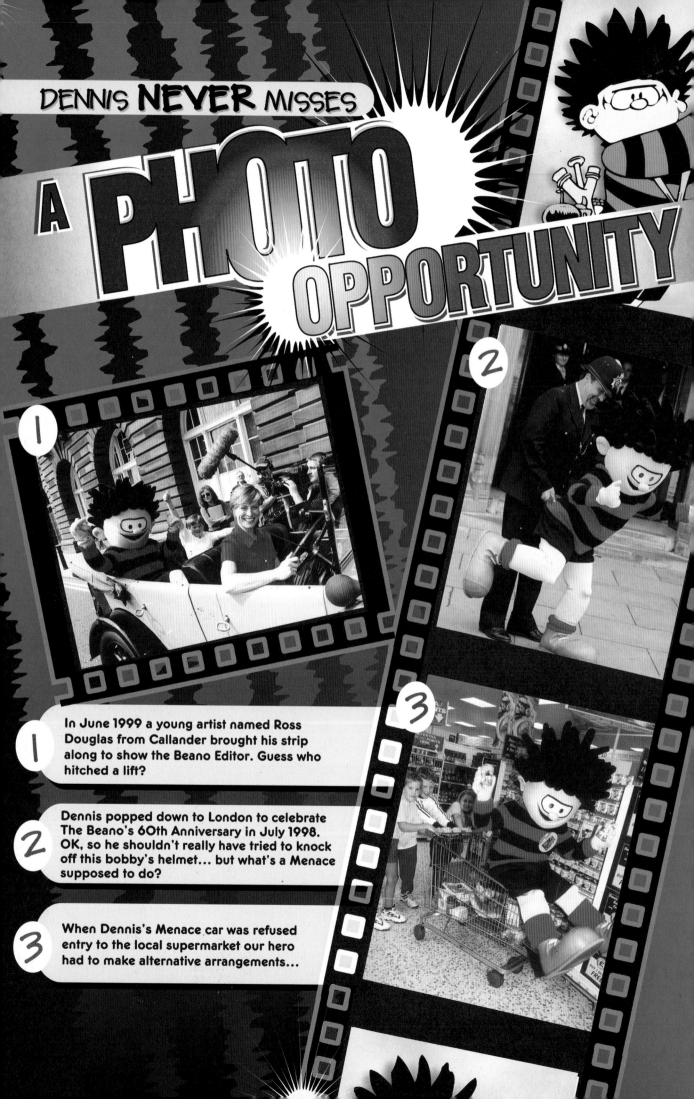

1. In June 1999 a young artist named Ross Douglas from Callander brought his strip along to show the Beano Editor. Guess who hitched a lift?

2. Dennis popped down to London to celebrate The Beano's 60th Anniversary in July 1998. OK, so he shouldn't really have tried to knock off this bobby's helmet... but what's a Menace supposed to do?

3. When Dennis's Menace car was refused entry to the local supermarket our hero had to make alternative arrangements...

DENNIS ACCORDING TO MUM

COOEE, EVERYONE! ONLY ME —
DENNIS'S MUM.
Let's have a nice cup of tea and a sticky bun
and we'll talk about my little boy.
Oo, he can be such a scamp, that boy of mine,
but I just put it down to high spirits.
He does make me laugh though, but Dad
slaps my face with a wet kipper and the
hysterics soon stop.
Anyway, enjoy my memories of Dennis. I do
hope my hair's not a mess when I appear.

*Dennis is a very nice, quiet, little chap
(when he's sleeping!)*

I'M AN AWARD WINNING MUM, YOU KNOW — THANKS TO DENNIS AND GNASHER. BY THE WAY, PLEASE DON'T LOOK AT ME IN MY CURLERS. OO! HOW EMBARRASSING!

7 a.m. —

OH, NO! ANOTHER DAY WITH MY AWFUL FAMILY!

DENNIS'S MUM

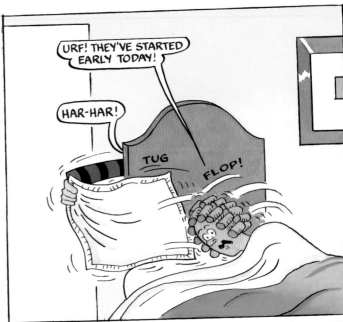

URF! THEY'VE STARTED EARLY TODAY!

HAR-HAR!

TUG

FLOP!

GREAT PILLOW FIGHT!

I'M FOREVER CLEARING UP BEHIND THEM.

AND MY VACUUM CLEANER SUCKS UP SO MUCH RUBBISH...

...IT'S GOT A WEIGHT PROBLEM!

STRAIN

BULGE

26th March, 198

Lunchtime—

CALCULATOR
BEEP!
BEEP!

DAD'S JUST AS BAD.

AW, MUM, DENNIS HAS GOT MORE PEAS THAN ME!

HERE—HAVE SOME!

SPLOT!
SPLAT!
TWANG!

LOOK AT THE STAINS ON MY SHIRT!

MUM'LL HAVE TO WASH IT.

BAH!

THEN THERE'S GNASHER...

EEK!

GNASH!
CRUNCH!

WHAT A FAMILY OF PESTS!

CHOMP!

Soon—

KNOCK!
KNOCK!

WHO'S THAT? SOMEONE COMPLAINING ABOUT DENNIS, NO DOUBT.

CONGRATULATIONS! YOU'VE WON OUR CONTEST!

BRITAIN'S TOP LONG-SUFFERING MUM

HERE'S YOUR PRIZE!

WE'LL HELP YOU EAT IT!

WHY SHOULD YOU GET ANY?

YOU COULDN'T HAVE WON IT WITHOUT US!

TRUE—VERY TRUE!

10th August, 19..

13th March, 198

4th August, 1962

DENNIS NEVER MISSES A PHOTO OPPORTUNITY

Dennis talks politics with Liberal Democrat leader Charles Kennedy. Here Dennis outlines his proposal for 51 weeks of school holidays.

When the Beanoland site opened at Chessington World of Adventures in April 2000 Beano Editor Euan Kerr was there to welcome everyone. Let's face it Euan - YOU'VE BEEN MENACED!!

AVAST, YE MENACES! COME ABOARD FOR A VOYAGE WITH ONE OF DENNIS'S ANCESTORS — A PIRATE ON THE SPANISH MAIN!

GNASHER ISLAND

IT'S RAINING OUTSIDE, SO YOU TWO CAN TIDY UP THE ATTIC!

AW, DAD!

COO! WONDER WHAT'S IN THIS OLD CHEST?

CORKS! IT'S THE LOG-BOOK OF THE PIRATE SHIP "VULTURE", WHICH SET SAIL TO SEEK TREASURE ON THE SPANISH MAIN IN 1582!

BACK TO THE YEAR 1582 —

YO-HO-HO, AND A BOTTLE OF POP!

THE PIRATE SHIP "VULTURE" IS OFF TO SEEK TREASURE!

Dennis the Menace Book, 1974

ON BOARD, THE SHIP'S DOG CHASES THE SHIP'S CAT —

GNASH!

LOOK — IT'S OLD SEA-DOG GNASHER, A DISTANT GRANDAD OF DENNIS'S PET!

COOK'S CABIN

THIS IS YOUNG JIM HAWK-NOSE, THE CABIN BOY!

THE TREASURE HUNT BEGINS —

AAR! TWENTY PACES EAST, ME BEAUTIES!

CAP'N STONE'S TREASURE MAP

WAIT FOR ME, YOU OLD SEA-DOG!

SNIFFSH!

YAHOO! WE'VE FOUND THE TREASURE! LET'S GET IT BACK TO THE SHIP, GNASHER!

AAR! AT LAST, ME BEAUTIE TEN MORE PACES AND—

I DIDN'T TAKE MY BOW (–WOW) TILL 31.8.68. BEFORE THAT DENNIS HAD A BIT OF A LAUGH WITH OTHER DOGS, AS YOU'LL SEE IN THE FOLLOWING PAGES.

DENNIS the MENACE

GET SCRUFFY, AN' GINGER'S SNAP, AN' ROVER, –AN' ALL THE GANG'S DOGS!

DOG SHOW
CITY HALL
PRIZES

BUT THESE ARE MONGRELS!

GIMME TIME–GIMME TIME–

LATER

–AN' A BOTTLE OF INK–THAT'S THE LOT!

INK

OWF! OWF! GR·RR! YELP!

DENNIS'S HUT!

HURRY UP – THE SHOW STARTS AT TWO–

AT THE SHOW

LOVELY DALMATION– LOVELY MARKINGS.

H'M'M'M!

INK!

SOME DACHSHUND– SOME LENGTH.

H'M'M'M–

TWO DOGS–AND A RUBBER TUBE!

SNAP!

POP!

H'M'M'M!

?

POODLES

COTTON WOOL!

DENNIS!

POODLES

THIS IS A DOG'S LIFE!

July, 1952

3rd October, 1953

with a CAT

GNORMALLY I'D NEVER USE SOFTY HAIRSPRAYS AND GELS, BUT WHEN IT'S IN A MENACING GOOD CAUSE, THERE'S GNO PROBLEM!

30th April, 1983

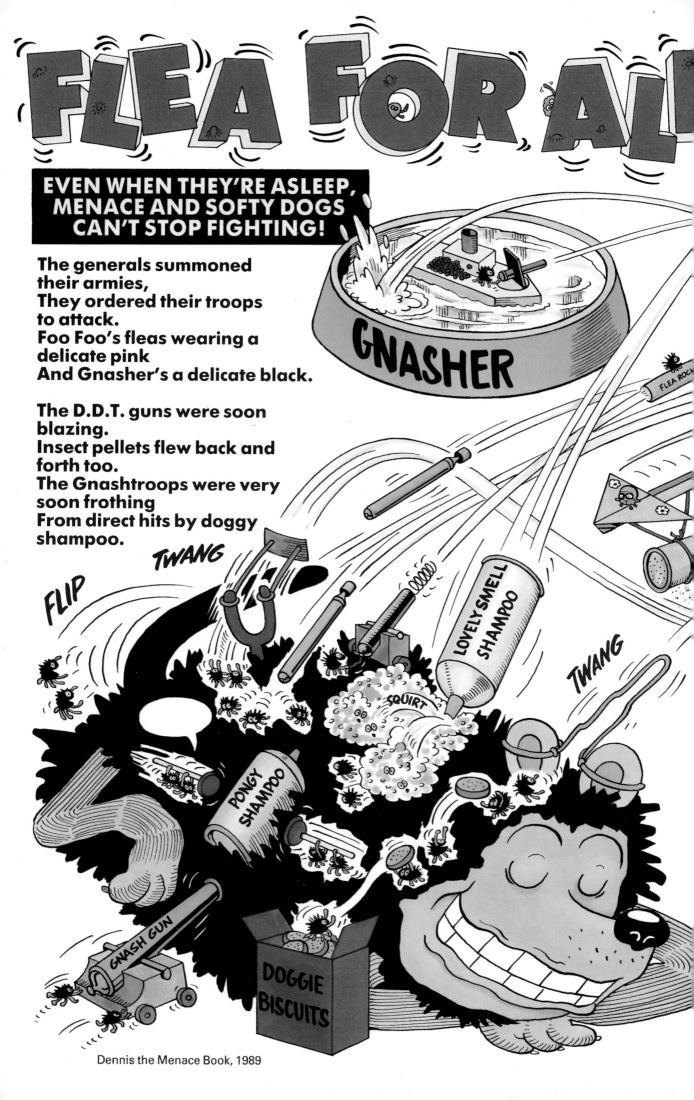

FLEA FOR ALL

EVEN WHEN THEY'RE ASLEEP, MENACE AND SOFTY DOGS CAN'T STOP FIGHTING!

The generals summoned
their armies,
They ordered their troops
to attack.
Foo Foo's fleas wearing a
delicate pink
And Gnasher's a delicate black.

The D.D.T. guns were soon
blazing.
Insect pellets flew back and
forth too.
The Gnashtroops were very
soon frothing
From direct hits by doggy
shampoo.

Dennis the Menace Book, 1989

In time, when our Gnasher
awakened.
He said, "What's been
going on here?
My tail is all twisted and
throbbing
There's elastic attached to
each ear."

"I know who's to blame, it
was Foo Foo."
He said with a fierce
sounding "Gurrr!"
So another fierce battle
soon started,
To resounding "Flea
Cheers!" from his fur.

GNOW AND THEN DENNIS STARTS A GNEW HOBBY. I WOULDN'T MIND BUT WHEN HE STARTED TO GNEGLECT ME — I'D HAD ENOUGH!

OH, GOODIE, MY BOOK!

"SWEET AND ADORABLE STORIES" FOR NICE LITTLE KIDDIES FROM THE BOOKCLUB

WALTER THE SOFTY

PAH! BORING OLD BOOKS!

GNESH!

STORIES FOR NICE LITTLE KIDDIES FROM THE BOOKCLUB

BOOK CLUB

VROOM!

I CAN'T WAIT TO START. I HOPE IT'S ANOTHER FAIRY STORY!

AAAGHH!

WHAT HAPPENED?

IF THIS MADE WALTER FAINT IT MUST BE GOOD!

URGLE! TAKE IT AWAY!

MONSTERS BOOK

WOW! WOW! WOW!

I'M STARVING!

RUMBLE! RUMBLE!

Much later—

OOOH! WHEN'S HE GOING TO TAKE ME HOME FOR LUNCH?

RUMBLE! RUMBLE!

HAR! HAR!

HO-HO!

CHUCKLE!

GURR! I'LL HAVE TO TAKE HIM HOME MYSELF!

1st June, 1985

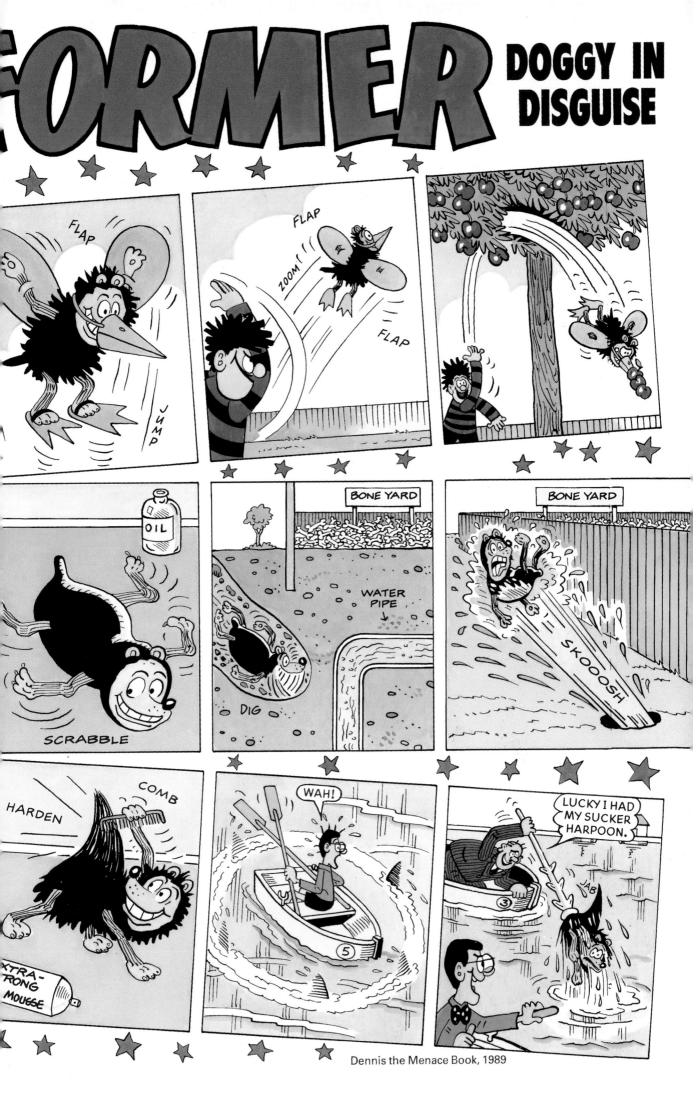

Dennis the Menace Book, 1989

IT'S GNICE TO BE WANTED, BUT NOT FOR BEING AN OUTLAW! GNEEK!

BACK HOME —

I'VE GOT THE VERY THING IN HERE, GNASHER!

TOY BOX

I'VE GOT A SUPER GUN-DOG FOR YOU, COLONEL BAGGE-SHOTT.

LET ME SEE IT, SMALL LAD.

HERE, GNASHER!

GNIPPEE, GNAIE!

12th October, 1974

A SHORT TALE

Dennis the Menace Book, 1974

Dennis the Menace Book, 1993

2nd October, 19

26th May, 198

9th June, 198

22nd December, 1962

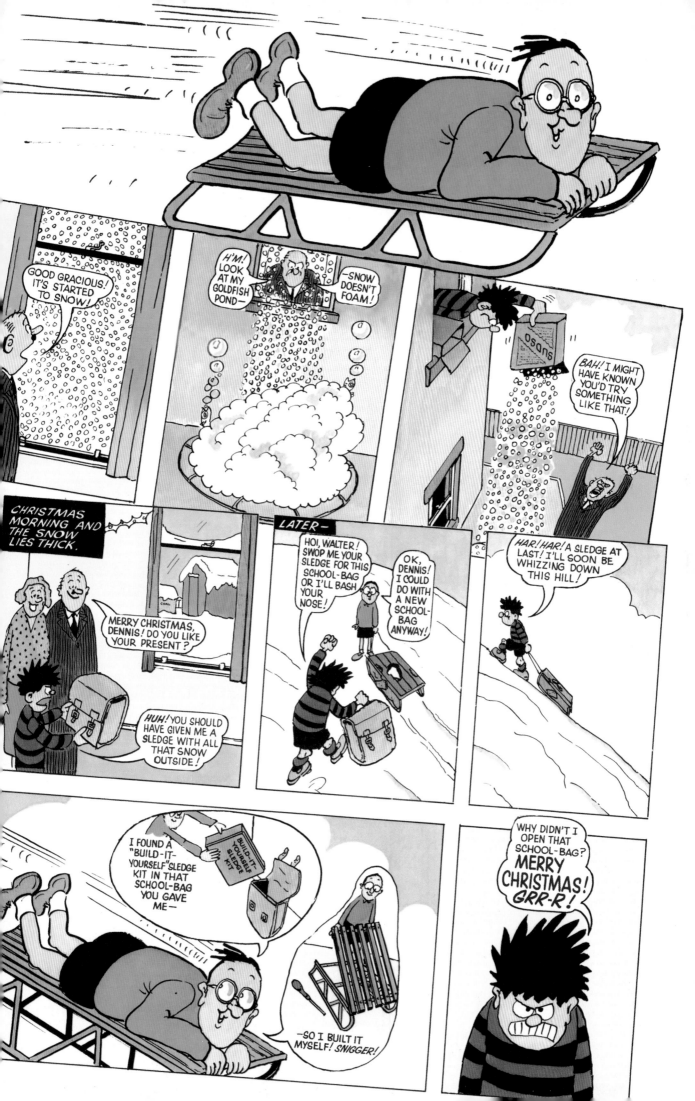

WHEN I'M OFF SCHOOL I HATE TO MISS A THING, SO I WAS VERY PLEASED WHEN DENNIS HELPED ME CATCH UP ON OUR CLASS ACTIVITIES. I SHOULD HAVE KNOWN BETTER!

SNIFFLE! I **HAD** TO STAY OFF SCHOOL TODAY— I HAD A WHOLE SNEEZE LAST NIGHT!

HMMM...

HI, GNASHER—SCHOOL HASN'T BEEN TOO AWFUL TODAY—WALTER THE SOFTY WAS OFF!

WOW! THEN YOU WON'T KNOW WHAT SPECIAL THING WE'RE DOING AT SCHOOL TOMORROW!

MAKING THIS UP

GOSH, NO! HARD SUMS? LONG ESSAYS? WHAT?

NONE OF THAT BORING STUFF. WE'RE HAVING A ROLF HARRIS PARTY!

OH, THAT AUSTRALIAN CHAPPIE ON CHILDREN'S TV!

WE'D BETTER GET YOU READY— EVERYONE ELSE WILL BE DRESSED LIKE ROLF TOMORROW...

TUG

OH, DEAR!

THERE!

DAB DAB

PAINT

HMM. NOT MUCH CHANCE OF Y GROWING A BEARD IN TIME...

OOER!

RUB

2nd February, 198

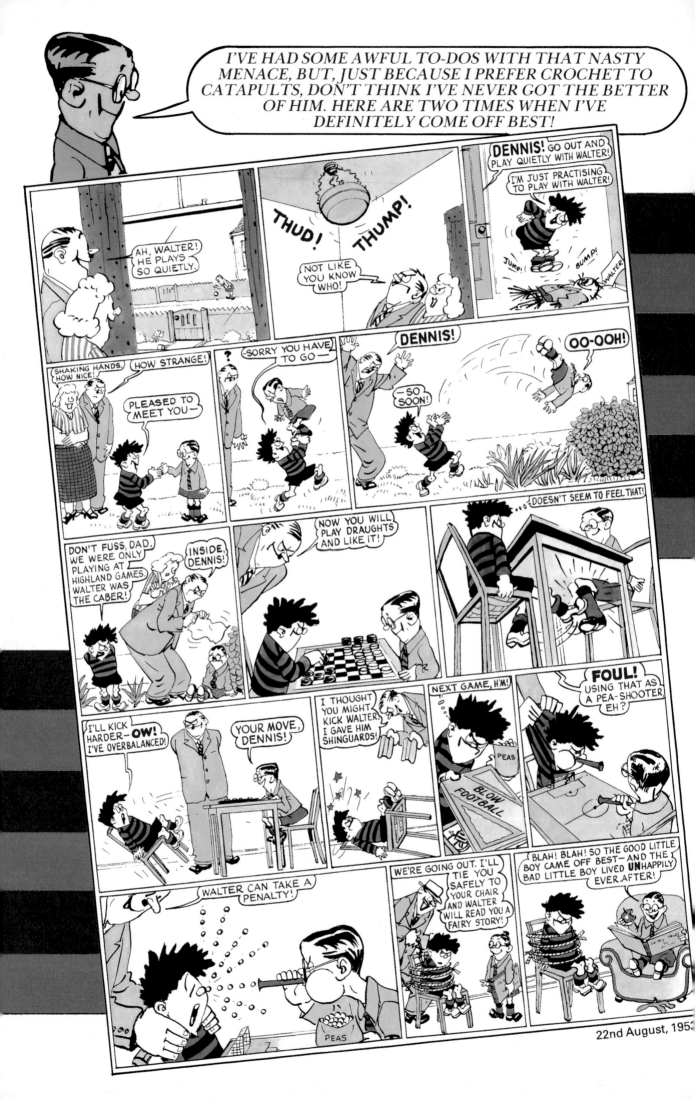

22nd August, 1953

14th November, 1953

6th November, 1982

Dennis the Menace Book, 1992

3rd September, 1983

CLOTHES PEGS! GET YOUR CLOTHES PEGS HERE — 5 PENCE EACH!

WHAT DO WE WANT CLOTHES PEGS FOR?

MUMS PEGS

CURRYISH NIFF

I'LL TAKE ONE!

ONE FOR ME!

AND ME!

NOW WE CAN AFFORD TO GO TO THE MATCH. BIG CROWD TODAY.

ROVERS v RANGERS

NO TROUBLE SEEING WHEN RASHER'S WITH US!

CURRY WAFT

POO!

Later—

AH! HOW BEAUTEOUS THE SNOWDROPS ARE!

SOFT SNIFF!

EEK!

STUNNING CURRY ODOUR

Later—

SWILL'S UP, RASHER.

SLURP!

GUZZLE! GLOOP!

I ADDED SOME ESSENCE OF VIOLETS!

ROTTEN TRICK!

GARGH!

OH, DEAR! MY AIR FRESHENER'S FINISHED.

NOT TO WORRY, MUM.

NICE NIFF

LAST DROP

RASHER MAKES A SUPER AIR-FRESHENER NOW!

LOVELY SMELL

SWEET VIOLET PONG

NICE AND WARM AGAIN!

February, 1983

18th July, 1981

PIG TALE

A LECTURE ON ZOOLOGY FROM RASHER, PROFESSOR OF PIGOLOGY AT ST TURNIPS COLLEGE, SOCKSFORD.

IT IS A WELL KNOWN FACT THAT ALL ANIMALS ARE DESCENDED FROM THE PIG.

The giraffe pig developed its long neck to eat from gutter pipes because they look remarkably like troughs.

The pig shark swims the oceans in search of turnips lost overboard from turnip tankers.

The lion pig is so powerful it can hunt down and catch a turnip 7 feet tall and weighing over 3 tons. unfortunately these do not exist any more . . .

. . . because all the elepha pigs ate them — and they' a huge appetite to feed yc know.

14th July, 1951

9th February, 1952

WE PLAY GREAT GAMES WITH DENNIS. ONLY TROUBLE IS, IF YOU PLAY WITH DENNIS, YOU GET IN TROUBLE WITH DENNIS . . . IF YOU FOLLOW ME!

GET THE BOYS, CURLY. WE'RE GOING TO PLAY "FOLLOW MY LEADER". I'LL BE THE LEADER!

RIGHT, LADS — DO AS I DO!

TAKE A SWEETIE, DENNIS!

TA, WALTER

TA, WALTER!

TA — SLURP! — WALTER!

AGGH! THE BAG'S EMPTY!

OH, BOY! IT'S BASHER BLOGGS, THE BULLY!

TAKE THAT!

TAKE THAT!

ZUNK!

DAZE

NICE DOGGIE!

PAT!

MUDDY PATCH

NICE DOGGIE!

PAT!

JIM, YOUR PRIZE RETRIEVER LOOKS LIKE A DACHSHUND AND I THINK I KNOW WHO'S BEHIND IT ALL

SU

RIGHT, DADS! — DO AS I DO!

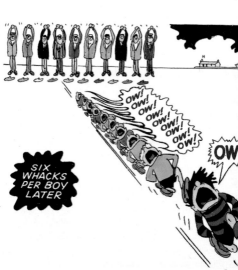

OW! OW! OW! OW! OW! OW!

OW!

SIX WHACKS PER BOY LATER

22nd July, 1961

YOU'VE HEARD OF "THE BODY SHOP" — WELL, DENNIS PLANS TO OPEN . . .

. . .THE BEASTIE SHOP

DAD

MENACE STYLE HEDGEHOG WIG

OCTOPUS DREADLOCK WIG

BERTIE BLENKINSOP

MOTH DUST EYE SHADOW

NERVOUS REX

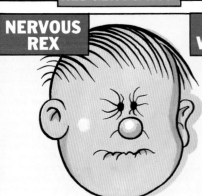

SPIDER LEG EYELASHES

SOFTY WALTER

SNAIL SLIME EYELID SOOTHERS

SPOTTY PERKINS

WORKER ANT SPOTS

CATERPILLAR EYEBROWS — AVAILABLE IN A VARIETY OF EXPRESSIONS

CURLY

THE "I'VE JUST BOUGHT A COPY OF THE BEANO" LOOK

PIE-FACE

THE "NO PIES LEFT" LOOK

MUM

THE "WHERE HAVE MY EYEBROWS GONE?" LOOK

7th February, 1

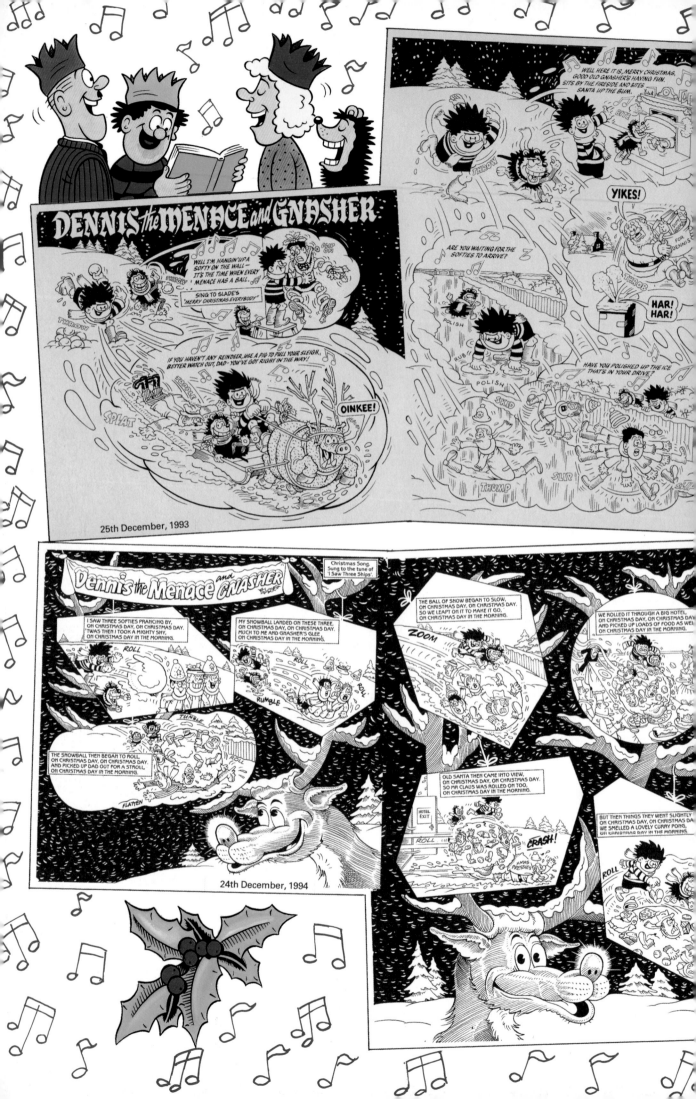

25th December, 1993

24th December, 1994

I'VE HAD ADVENTURES OF MY OWN TOO, YOU GNOW. I REMEMBER ONE COLD NIGHT, I WENT

PUP, PUP and AWAY!

IT was to be the coldest night in Beanotown for many a year. It was so cold that Jack Frost was tucked up in his ice house, with frostbite. "It's blooming freezing out there," he said, chillingly.

BLOW!

FREEZING WIND
ICY BLAST

Gnasher's teeth chattered as he lay in his kennel. "Terrible weather we're having!" said one. "I could do with a dog biscuit," said another. "Shut up!" Gnasher ordered his choppers. The biting wind howled in through the cracks in his kennel and Gnasher howled out through the cracks in his lips. He hadn't been this cold since he swallowed an icicle he'd mistaken for a bone.

At that moment, the wind reached full strength (it had been working out in the gym) and Gnasher and his kennel were swept into the air. Gnasher was terrified . . . GRROWL! (Okay, okay! Gnasher was only slightly worried — Editor) as the wind bore him and his kennel out to sea.

WHEEEEE!

GNASHER

All the creatures of the deep were amazed as the kennel flew past and shouted their greetings to Gnasher. A dogfish threw him a bone for breakfast and even the waves waved.

ZOOM!

GRAB

WAVE

FLIP

WAVE

WHEEE!

SHAVE

BZZZZ!

Gnasher was still cold, so he had a heated conversation with a seagull. When the conversation started to get out of hand, they decided to shake and make up. Gnasher quite liked shaking — it kept him warm. But he did look pretty stupid with make up on.

By now the wind was dropping faster than a toothless man with laryngitis could say, "Two tickets to Tooting"! Within eight hours it died away completely!

The kennel floated gently down on to a strange tropical beach of purple and yellow sand. Gnasher was covered in a strange mixture of both. "I've been marooned!" he said. "Is this island uninhabited or does nobody live here?" he wondered. As if in answer to his question, a familiar smell reached his nostrils. (actually, it reached his tail first and had to ask a flea for directions).

WHEEE!

FLUMP

"Gnippee! I smell postmen!" Gnasher set off down the beach like a greyhound. He couldn't keep up the impersonation however and ran on like the Wire-haired Abyssinian Tripe Hound he really was.

A fabulous sight greeted Gnasher's eyes. "Hello, Gnasher's eyes!" it said. As far as his ears could see, the beach was covered by sunbathing posties.

"I've found the legendary lost island of retired postmen!" Gnasher was filling up with excitement. (There was a handy self-service "excitement" station nearby).

Eventually, he fell into a deep, contented sleep and dreamt of doing it all again tomorrow. The posties had other ideas!

TWANG!
Gnasher was fired into the air and was caught by the wind. (It had been learning cricket as well as working out in the gym).

The wind carried the sleeping Gnasher back to Beanotown, back to the Menace house and in through Dennis' bedroom window.

After a few gallons of lead-free five star excitement, he dived into the middle of a group of panicking posties! Nipping a rear here, biting a trouser leg there, he ran himself off his feet, his ankles and his knees chasing them across the beach.

They picked up the slumbering Gnasher and placed him on the end of a palm tree they had bent back to form a catapult . . .

When Gnasher woke up in the morning, he thought he'd been dreaming, but no-one ever did explain what happened to his kennel or why he had a lovely sun tan in the middle of January!

TANK

7th October, 1961

I'M NOT A BAD LAD, JUST MISUNDERSTOOD! WHEN BEANOTOWN WAS HUNTIN' FOR A MODEL YOUNG CITIZEN, I KNEW I WAS . .

IDEAL BOY CONTEST!
WHO WILL BE THE TOWN'S IDEAL BOY? HE MUST BE QUIET — INDUSTRIOUS — INTELLIGENT — AND KIND TO HIS PARENTS.
VOTING WILL TAKE PLACE AT THE TOWN HALL TODAY.

I'M QUIET —

— ESPECIALLY IN THE HISTORY CLASS

BLAH – BLAH.... 1066....

Z-Z-Z!

CAKE TIN

— BECAUSE I HAVE A LARGE COLLECTION OF TEXT BOOKS WHICH I USE A LOT!

SHAKESPEARE
ANCIENT HISTORY
GRAMMER
ENCYCLOPEDIA
GREEK
LATIN
GEOMETRY
ARITHMETIC

I'M ALSO KIND TO MY PARENTS —

— FOR INSTANCE —

EEK!

TO DAD FROM DENNIS

HAPPY FATHER'S DAY

COTTON WOOL SOLE!

HAPPY MOTHER'S DAY FROM DENNIS

THEN SUDDENLY DENNIS APPEARS —

AGH-H! IT'S THE MENACE!

NOISE METER

GOOD
FAIR
DEAR BOY
LITTLE ANGEL
DISGUSTING
IDEAL BOY

GOOD GRACIOUS! THE MACHINE SAYS THAT DREADFUL URCHIN IS THE "IDEAL BOY"!

THE ORGANISER ISN'T VERY POPULAR WITH THE FOND MAMMAS —

MY DEAR LITTLE WATTY SHOULD HAVE WON!

ZONK!

HAW! HAW!

LADIES, PLEASE! IT WAS THE NOISE METER'S FAULT — NOT MINE!

THE IDEAL BOY

14th July, 1962

23rd January, 1954

GNASHER'S NOT THE ONLY ANIMAL I'VE MENACED WITH. HERE COME A FEW TALES OF ANIMAL ANTICS FOR YOU TO ENJOY, STARTING WITH MY CAPERS WITH A CAMEL!

11th November, 1961

 MONKEY

THE CIRCUS IS IN TOWN—

BINGO'S

OUT! AND DON'T LET ME CATCH YOU TRYING TO SNEAK IN HERE AGAIN!

THUD!

HUH! HE WON'T KEEP THE MENACE OUT FOR LONG!

THEN—

MATHS BOOK

GOSH! IT'S ALGY, THE EDUCATED APE! I'VE GOT AN IDEA!

YOU'LL DO AS I SAY MONKEY— OR ELSE!

SEE ALGY THE EDUCATED APE AT BINGO'S CIRCUS HE'S ALMOST HUMAN

BINGO'S CIRCUS

HEY-HO! IN I GO!

BUT—

WHERE HAVE YOU BEEN, ALGY? YOU'RE ON NEXT!

ERK!

SNATCH

AT DENNIS'S HOUSE—

BASH! BASH!

ANGRY

ERK! IT'S DAD!

HAH! DENNIS! I MIGHT HAVE GUESSED IT WAS YOU!

SMUG

BUSINESS

AH! THE COUNTRYSIDE! LOTS OF MEADOW FULL OF LOVELY FLOWERS: LAMBS FROLICKI IN THE GRASS ... JUST THE PLACE TO CAL DENNIS DOWN, DON'T YOU THINK? NO? OH WELL, MAYBE NOT ...

DENNIS IS STAYING WITH HIS GRANNY IN THE COUNTRY —

NOW DON'T GET UP TO MISCHIEF!

SNAP!

BUT SOON DENNIS IS UP TO MISCHIEF — PRETTY HIGH MISCHIEF TOO! —

THERE GOES GRANNY'S PATCH!

TEAR!

TOO BAD YOUNG FELLOW-ME-LAD! YOU'VE WASTED A PAIR OF TROUSERS THERE ISN'T ANYTHING EXCITING THIS SIDE OF THE FENCE!

CAN YOU PATCH M AGAIN, GRAN

I WANT YOU TO TAKE AN URGENT MESSAGE TO FARMER JONES, BUT I MUST CHANGE YOUR PATCH FIRST!

DENNIS STARTS OUT ACROSS THE FIELDS —

FARM FROLICS

THAT'S TORN IT!

GRANNY, HAVE YOU A MINUTE TO DO A SPOT OF PATCHING?

LATER—

OHO! THERE'S ALWAYS SOMETHING INTERESTING BEHIND BARBED WIRE!

LATER—

COO-HOO! DENNIS!

I'M TOO BUSY TO PAY ATTENTION TO GRANNY!

COME HERE!

WHIZZ!

BONK!

SOAP

THE BULL SEES RED AND HELPS HIM ON HIS WAY!

THANKS FOR DELIVERING THAT MESSAGE IN A HURRY, DENNIS!

12th May, 1956

10th November, 1962

ALL THE GOOD JOBS HAVE GONE! MODERN CAREERS LIKE COMPUTERS AND THE INTERNET ARE NO GOOD FOR ME, BUT THE CARE-FREE LIFE OF A HIGHWAYMAN? ... MENACE HEAVEN!

COME BACK! I WANT TO WASH YOUR FACE!

BRUMM!

HEE! HEE! MY TRAP WORKED!

BUT, MUM, I'M DENNIS TURPENTINE, THE DREADED HIGHWAYMAN!

QUIET!

FRESHLY SCRUBBED, DENNIS SETS OUT IN SEARCH OF ADVENTURE—AND LAUGHS!

AHA! FIRST VICTIM!

HOLD, VARLET! STAND—

FLICK

—AND DELIVER! HEH! HEH!

HUP, BESS, MY BEAUTY!

IMAGINARY HORSE

MY LOVELY COLD-FRAME!

CRASH!

OH, NO! NOW HE'S RUINED MY NEW CEMENT PATH!

ONWARD, BESS!

DOVER

AHA! NOW TO HOLD UP THE DOVER COACH!

STAND AND—

YES?

GLUG!

OH! OH! IT'S THAT GARDENER!

10 HOLD-UPS LATER, HE GOES HOME.

I'M ALMOST CERTAIN IT WAS DENNIS, BUT HE WAS WEARING A MASK.

SO IT WAS YOU WHO DAMAGED THIS MAN'S PROPERTY!

INNOCENCE

YOU CAN'T PROVE IT, DAD!

OH, CAN'T I? IF YOU LOOK IN THE MIRROR YOU'LL SEE AN UGLY FACE COVERED WITH OIL—EXCEPT WHERE THE MASK WAS!

ERK!

SMIRK

23rd June, 1956

INSTEAD OF BREAKING THE LAW, I BET I'D BE GREAT AT CATCHING MENACES. AFTER ALL, I KNOW ALL THE INSIDE INFO!

HOW DO YOU LIKE MY NEW DOG, DENNIS?

HMM! IT WOULD MAKE A GOOD BLOODHOUND— AND I'D MAKE A GOOD DETECTIVE.

DENNIS THE DETECTIVE IS SOON HOT ON THE TRAIL—

LOOK AT THOSE BLOODSTAINS, CURLY!

—BUT A SHOCK AWAITS HIM.

ERK! IT'S JAM!

GRRR!

LATER.

I CAN TELL YOU THAT THE BOY WHO MADE THOSE FOOTPRINTS HAD HAM AND EGG FOR HIS BREAKFAST, BROKE A WINDOW THIS MORNING AND GOT TEN WHACKS FROM A SLIPPER THIS AFTERNOON!

THAT'S MARVELLOUS, DENNIS! HOW CAN YOU TELL ALL THAT?

ELEMENTARY, MY DEAR CURLY. I MADE THOSE FOOTPRINTS HALF AN HOUR AGO!

LATER.

SOMEBODY'S STOLEN YOUR SWEETS, EH? NEVER MIND, M'BOY. THE GREAT DENNIS AN' HIS NOBLE HOUND WILL TRACK DOWN THE THIEF!

WAH!

C'M'ON, YOU! PICK UP THE SCENT!

AT LAST!

SCENT

SNIFF!

ONE MAD DASH LATER.

BAH! HE WAS ONLY FOLLOWING THE SCENT OF THAT PIE!

HAR! HAR! SOME POOR MUG WON'T BE GETTING ANY DINNER!

BUT THEN THE OWNER OF THE PIE APPEARS.

ARRGH! IT'S MUM!

GRRR! GO HOME AND TAKE THAT USELESS HOUND WITH YOU!

SHAME

NOW, LET'S SEE, MAYBE THERE'S A CRUMB OF PIE LEFT FOR MY DINNER!

18th February, 1961

19th November, 1960

24th November, 195

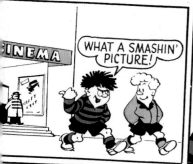

th November, 1951

3rd January, 1953

DENNIS NEVER MISSES A PHOTO OPPORTUNITY

NOR DOES GNASHER!

Dennis and Gnasher team up with fellow mischief-lover Gazza to seek out the UK's Mega Menace. Gnasher was keen to show the England star his bite-your-leg tackles.

Who better than toothy terror Gnasher to help *Vets in Practice* star Trude Mostue launch Pet Smile Month in February 2000? Gnasher didn't even mind that Trude hadn't brought along his usual wire toothbrush.

21st July, 1951

12th November, 1983

28th February, 19

3rd September, 1961

50 Years

I'm Dennis gondolier

FREE INSIDE THE HAPPY HOWLER SIREN!

The BEANO

No. 1678—SEP. 14th, 1974. EVERY THURSDAY 3p

DENNIS THE MENACE AND GNASHER

Dennis and Gnasher pinch the front cover for the first time.

...So went the music hall song which was heard by the first Beano editor, George Moonie, and which was the inspiration behind the christening of Dennis the Menace — The World's Wildest Boy, who first misbehaved in The Beano issue dated March 17th, 1951.

The little, spiky-haired terror has changed the face of many things in his time, including big hair rugby players, ruthless commandos and huge wrestlers but his arrival at the start of the 1950's changed the face of British comics.

Up until that time the traditional comics were populated by a cosy mix of cute animal characters such as Big Eggo the Ostrich, Korky the Cat and Biffo the Bear or fantasy– based strips like Jimmy and his Magic Patch, Ping the Elastic Man or Tin Can Tommy, the Clockwork Boy.

Dennis was completely different — he was high-spirited and naughty (VERY naughty) and the funny (VERY funny) thing was that the more rebellious and mischievous Dennis became, the more the readers loved him.

He took the comic by storm and there was

Below: Selected Dennis the Menace Book covers.

1956

1958

1960

♪ Menace from Venice, a gay ♪
n gold rings in my ear . . . . ♪

o stopping him.
From being
allocated a half-
page black and
white strip on his
debut, he added
limited colour (red),
then grabbed the full-
colour back page of The Beano.

Dennis was on a roll and then
chanced upon a stray
Abyssinnian Wire-haired
Tripehound in August, 1968.
Impressed by the hound's
granite-shattering teeth, Dennis
called the beast Gnasher. Like
Laurel and Hardy, Tom and Jerry,
Morecambe and Wise, Dennis
and Gnasher became one of the
great comic teams.

With Gnasher's help, Dennis
went from strength to strength.
His popularity became so great
that in 1974 he not only launched

the
incredibly
successful
Dennis the
Menace Fan Club
(including Gnasher's Fang Club)
but he also gave Biffo the Bear
the elbow
from the coveted cover slot of
The Beano.

The Fan Club enrolled
members faster than Billy Whizz

with his
pants on fire
and in 1988 the millionth Fan
Club member signed up for his
membership kit which included
the famous hairy Gnasher badge
with moving eyes.

Simon Palmer (the millionth
member) flew up to visit Dennis

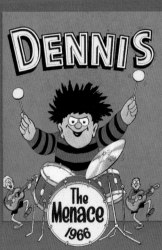

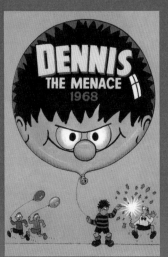

Robert Harrop Designs Ltd. produce a very popular range of collectable figures, including the Menace Car.

in The Beano headquarters in Dundee. As well as a traditional comic feed, Simon was presented with a huge array of goodies, as by now our hero had started to pop up on all sorts of merchandise from boxer shorts to bedding.

Dennis was no longer just a comic star — a puppet version of Dennis and Gnasher were up to mischief in their own show on The Children's Channel. After starring in two animated videos, "The Beano Video!" and "Beano Videostars", Dennis was offered a television deal and the chance to Menace some new victims — The Colonel, Sergeant Slipper and Walter's girlfriend Matilda — in a series which topped the ratings on both the BBC and Fox Kids.

Just to show that he's not all bad, Dennis has been involved in a Say No To Strangers campaign, a Help Beat The Menace cancer charity initiative as well as featuring in a Menca money-raiser.

As this book has shown, Dennis the Menace has changed in many ways during the past fifty years. One thing has never changed though . . . HE'S STILL THE WORLD'S WILDEST BOY!

Royal Doulton's version of The Menace, and a selection of Dennis products.

Simon Palmer, the millionth member of The Dennis the Menace Fan Club, meets his hero.

3rd June, 1961

CONGRATULATIONS –
It's A Menace!

September, 1998. Beanotown holds its breath, fearing the worst. Dennis's Mum is expecting another baby — but is the world ready for Dennis Mk. II?

A few weeks earlier, Dennis knew *something* was up. A Dennis and the Dinmakers riot... sorry, concert... was abandoned because Mum was feeling poorly (not because of the music, which was a change) and wanted to lie down. Dad was more stressed-out than usual, and even Gnasher could sense something was about to happen.

Then Dad decided to decorate the spare bedroom. Dennis's paintbomb scheme (in contrasting red and black — move over, Laurence Llewellyn Bowen!) was rejected in favour of Softy wallpaper. Dennis was getting worried, and when Walter arrived carrying a suitcase, he knew his worst fears had been realised — Walter was coming to stay!

He needn't have worried — Walter was just doing some softy stencilling for Dad. Mighty relieved, Dennis confronted his parents. Either tell him what was going on or he'd QUIT THE BEANO!!!

In his absence, various incompetents tried to fill the famous jersey. Frustrated by their absolute uselessness, Dennis returned, demanding to know the big secret. So Mum and Dad told him: he was going to have a baby brother or sister!

When he came round, he realised he should have guessed. After all, why else would Mum knit baby clothes and try them on Gnipper? Or Dad practice putting nappies on Gnasher? (Bad idea, that!) And just as he was getting used to the idea...

His fears soon proved groundless: the baby was a bundle of mischief — just like her brother!

One more thing was still to be settled — what to call the new arrival? The family were stumped. Visitors to The Beano's web-site came to the rescue and christened her 'Bea'.

Dennis and Bea — what a team!

The Dennis the Menace Book, 1956

I'VE HAD TWO TV SERIES OF MY OWN, BUT BEFORE THAT I HAD TO MAKE DO WITH ORDINARY TELLY. HERE'S A DAY'S VIEWING FROM 1992. TURN ON, TUNE IN . . . AND MENACE!

TODAY'S TELEVISION PROGRAMMES AT A GLANCE

MENACE TV

6.30 BREAKFAST TV
Anne Diamond reports on Dennis's attempts to smash the "Most Things Broken with a Catapult" record. (Watch your teeth, Anne!)

9.25 AFTER NINE
Dennis shows you lots of different ways to arrive late at school.

9.45 RAINBOW
Bungle, George and Zippy are joined by special guests Gnasher and Gnipper.

10.00 SEWING MASTERCLASS
Walter shows you how to patch and repair furry TV puppets destroyed by fierce black dogs.

10.30 NEWS AND WEATHER
Mum and Mrs O'Reilly next door discuss the state of Dad's bunion, the rising price of sprouts and how chilly it is for the time of year.

10.50 NEIGHBOURS AWAY
Menace TV's answer to Neighbours and Home and Away. In today's episode, the entire community leaves when Dennis drops a twenty megapong stink-bomb.

11.00 ANTIQUES ROADSHOW
Dennis's Granny and her cronies go out for a morning drive.

12.00 CLIMBWATCH
An update of Dennis's progress on his way up Walter's Apple tree.

12.30 MASH
Cookery tips as Dad gets the spuds ready for lunch.

1.00 FILM — HAMLET
Rasher stars in this remake of the Shakespearian classic.

3.00 RACING FROM MENACETOWN
Brough Scott brings you commentary on today's Hunters Chase when lots of angry gents with shotguns pursue Gnasher for scaring off all the pheasants and partridges in the area.

5.00 ALL SCREECHERS GREAT AND SMALL
Walter and his Soprano Choir give a recital of arias. (Warning — remove all crystal glasses from the room before tuning in.)

6.00 IT'S A KNOCK OUT
Jeremy Beadle makes the mistake of trying out one of his little tricks on Dennis. (Last in the present series).

7.00 THE BILL
Dad counts the cost of Dennis's visit to the glass factory.

8.00 CLOSEDOWN
Sorry, viewers — Dennis has been sent to bed without any supper.

THERE'S ONLY SO MUCH MENACING YOU CAN DO IN ONE DAY, SO IT'S VITAL TO USE EVERY MINUTE YOU CAN. THAT'S WHY MY DREAMS ARE SWEET TO ME — AND NIGHTMARES FOR EVERYONE ELSE!

WHEN DAY IS DONE

At night time my Dad yells at me, '' It's time you're bedded, Dennis.''
He thinks that once I'm tucked in bed I cease to be a menace.
That's where he's wrong. Believe me, chums, I find I really make
A bigger menace fast asleep—than when I'm wide awake.

I DREAM I'm Davy Crockett, the man who shows no fear.
The roughest, toughest fighter on the Indian frontier.
I fight the Injuns my own way. You ought to know me, chaps.
I catch 'em in the forest with my special booby traps.

I DREAM that I'm a pirate in a special pirate suit.
My crew are armed with catapults and loads of rotten fruit.
And when I make folk walk the plank I shout out, '' Dance, you lubber.''
And watch 'em bouncing up and down on planks made out of rubber.

I DREAM that I'm King Alfred out hunting for the foe.
And, like King Alf, at baking cakes I really have a go.
The extra-special cakes I bake I give 'em to the Danes,
And have 'em quickly in retreat with stomach aches and pains.

I DREAM that I'm Napoleon with an army at my back.
With a thousand heavy cannon I am ready to attack.
But I've loaded every cannon with a super, large-sized tack!
That's how I win my battles, chaps. No kidding. It's a fac'.

I DREAM that I'm exploring in the drifting desert sand.
I dream that I'm a famous spy in a far-off foreign land.
My dreams they last the whole night through—but always end the same.
You've guessed it—Dad keeps popping up to stop my little game!

WAKE UP, DENNIS!

The Dennis the Menace Book, 195

O is for Opera. My, what a din!

P is for Pot Shot. See Denn grin.

Q is for Queuers—all in a row.

R is for Roller Skates. Down they all go!

S is for Slippers—warming for Dad!

T is for Temptation to burn them—that's BAD!